IMAGES
of America

HISTORIC INNS
OF ASHEVILLE

The Asheville Hotel, located at the corner of Haywood and Walnut Streets, is seen here. (D.H. Ramsey Library Special Collections, E.M. Ball Collection.)

IMAGES
of America

HISTORIC INNS
OF ASHEVILLE

Amy C. Ridenour

ARCADIA
PUBLISHING

Published by Arcadia Publishing
Charleston, South Carolina

Printed in the United States of America

Library of Congress Control Number: 2013931867

For all general information, please contact Arcadia Publishing:
Telephone 843-853-2070
Fax 843-853-0044
E-mail sales@arcadiapublishing.com
For customer service and orders:
Toll-Free 1-888-313-2665

Visit us on the Internet at www.arcadiapublishing.com

*To my parents, who always supported my love of history and
anything else that interested me; and to my husband, Kris,
who helped in so many ways to make this book happen*

CONTENTS

ACKNOWLEDGMENTS

My thanks go out to Elaine Blake and the Western North Carolina Historical Society for sparking my interest in Asheville's history.

Katie McAlpin, my acquisitions editor at Arcadia, was instrumental in bringing about the final idea for this book. Thank you!

Hidden down a hallway in the basement of Asheville's Pack Library is a special place: the North Carolina Collection Room. I found a wealth of information there that was carefully archived and easily accessible. Thank-yous go to Zoe Rhine, for helping me get started looking through articles and directories for information on tourism in Asheville; Lyme Kedic, for showing me how to use the digital archives and answering a million other questions; and Betsy Murray, for sending me dozens of great photographs.

A thank-you also goes to Laura Gardner at UNC Asheville's Ramsey Library for helping me get photographs, especially from its extensive Grove Park Inn collection.

A big thank-you goes not only to the Pack and Ramsey Libraries, who have collected, preserved, and archived these histories, but also to the photographers who left behind a legacy of photographs for us not only to enjoy, but also to learn from. These photographers include but are not limited to Ewart Ball Sr., Ewart Ball Jr., John B. Robinson, George Masa, John D. Caldwell, Herbert Pelton, and Andrea Clark.

Multiple writers helped me along the way with their works as well, including Bruce E. Johnson, who has done a spectacular job documenting the history of the Grove Park Inn in his books, including *Built for the Ages* and *Tales of the Grove Park Inn*, and Richard D. Starnes, whose book *Creating the Land of the Sky* started my research in this area.

There cannot be enough thanks for a husband like Kris, who is so generous and a never-ending supporter of mine.

Unless otherwise noted, the images in this volume appear courtesy of the Pack Memorial Library in Asheville, from its North Carolina Collection (Pack); the D.H. Ramsey Library Special Collections, UNC Asheville, from the E.M. Ball Collection (Ball) and the Grove Park Inn Collection (GPI); or the author (Author).

INTRODUCTION

In the 1790s, Buncombe County, North Carolina, was often referred to as the "State of Buncombe" because it encompassed so much land, stretching from Tennessee to Georgia and the Upstate of South Carolina. In 1793, Morristown became the seat of Buncombe County, and in 1797 was renamed Asheville to honor Samuel Ashe, who was the governor of North Carolina at the time. Asheville sat high in the mountains, at the confluence of two foot trails previously used by Cherokee and traders.

At first an isolated town of just a few hundred people, Asheville was an important stop for drovers taking their animals by foot to market from Greeneville, Tennessee, to Greenville, South Carolina, in the late fall. When this road was formally organized and improved into the Buncombe Turnpike in 1828, it became a major thoroughfare. Drover's stands began to appear along the turnpike—the first inns of Asheville. The local population created an industry catering to the needs of the drovers, making money feeding and lodging the drovers and their animals.

By the mid-1800s, planters from the Lowcountry of South Carolina began to visit Asheville during the summer months to escape the muggy heat of their plantations. Stagecoaches ran along Buncombe Turnpike, bringing visitors who could afford to stay for weeks and months in the cooler climate of the mountains.

In 1882, the railroad finally broke through the rugged mountain terrain, making Asheville more accessible and more popular than ever. With the trains came wealthy people from northern cities looking to escape the cold winters, as well as people from farther south traveling to the cool, beautiful mountains in the summer. The population of the city quadrupled in the 1880s, from 2,600 to more than 10,000, with another 50,000 people visiting the city annually. With Asheville already home to six hotels in 1880, several more opened during the ensuing decade. The Battery Park, the Swannanoa, the Victoria Inn, Margo Terrace, the Kenilworth, and the Glen Rock all represented the Victorian opulence and leisurely welcome guests expected at the time.

Since the late 1700s, the restorative climate and healing mountain air has brought people looking for health cures to Asheville, and the accessibility brought on by the railroad helped facilitate its reputation as a health resort. Famous doctors offered treatments for tuberculosis and other lung diseases at sanitariums, and luxury hotels offered a fashionable place to recover from social exhaustion. Ambler Heights, Winyah, Dr. Carroll's, and Ottari Sanitariums were some of the most famous places to receive treatment in their time.

Forward-thinking people who were settling in the steadily growing town began to realize that there was a lucrative business in catering to the growing classes of visitors. Many prominent citizens and visitors, including James Patton, George Vanderbilt, Col. Frank Coxe, and E.W. Grove, saw value in building inns and hotels that would provide guests with a comfortable place to sleep and meals to satisfy diverse palates. Many residents opened their houses to visitors; at one time, Asheville boasted over 100 boardinghouses in the city directory, the most famous of which, the Old Kentucky Home, was immortalized in Thomas Wolfe's novel *Look Homeward, Angel*. All of the town's founding families were once visitors, and the population continued to grow as tourists became locals over the decades. Those who did not make money running an inn or boardinghouse found employment as waiters, bellmen, domestics, cooks, laundresses, tour guides, chauffeurs, stable hands, bricklayers, or one of the countless other jobs created by the tourism industry.

Early purveyors of Asheville's tourism industry were not shy about promoting their mountain town. Advertisements and souvenir pamphlets were distributed widely, touting the beauty and the climate of the "Land of the Sky," where "every season is delightful" and "hospitality is a tradition." The term "Land of the Sky" was first used in a novel of that name written by Christian Reid in 1896, which itself reads like an advertisement for tourism in the area. A later novel, *Azure-Lure*, was commissioned by local businesses and chambers of commerce to promote Asheville as the perfect place to visit.

The demands of visiting guests led city leaders to improve the infrastructure of the city through more modern roads, water, and electrical lines. The Battery Park, opened in 1886, was the first grand hotel built in Asheville, one of the first in the South with electric lamps, and the first to have an Otis elevator. Another large hotel, the Swannanoa, quickly added the first bathroom in Asheville, to meet the demands of guests used to such amenities outside of the mountains. Asheville boasted one of the earliest and best streetcar systems in the nation—at one time operating 45 trolleys on 18 miles of track—allowing visitors who traveled into town by railway to get around town with ease, as streetcars passed in front of hotels at regular intervals.

After World War I, the growing prosperity of the country was reflected in Asheville. Multiple new hotels were built, including a new Kenilworth and Battery Park, the Grove Park Inn, the George Vanderbilt, and the Asheville-Biltmore Hotel. These hotels were the center of social life for Asheville and continued to bring in a multitude of visitors, especially from northern cities such as New York and Philadelphia, which were less than a day's train ride away. Although automobiles were starting to become popular throughout the United States, major highways had not yet been created to make Asheville easily accessible by road, but they were in the works.

The Great Depression hit Asheville hard, in part due to the large amounts of money the city spent on improvements such as parks and recreation, which were aimed at attracting more visitors. Tourism slowed through the 1930s, and the population of Asheville between 1930 and 1950 only grew from 50,193 to 53,000.

Everything changed for the better after World War II. Travel shifted from railways to highways, and the popularity of the automobile, along with the opening of tourist attractions such as the Biltmore Estate, Great Smoky Mountains National Park, and the Blue Ridge Parkway, made Asheville more popular than ever. The interstate highway system through the mountains was completed in 1966, just a few years after the regional airport opened in 1961. Families made their way through the mountains and filled the motels—now equipped with heated pools and television sets—that dotted the highways leading to Asheville.

The inns of Asheville have hosted millions of guests, from animal drovers to presidents, arriving by stagecoach or station wagon,. Some came for the beauty and peace of the mountains, some came because they were sick and they felt the city would heal them, and some came just because it was the fashionable place to go. Many of the inns, hotels, and motels still exist today, often showing No Vacancy signs during the busy summer months and the even-busier "leaf-peeping" season in the fall. Asheville still holds all of its charms for the young and the old, the sick and the healthy, the wealthy and the vagabond, those looking to find themselves and those looking to lose themselves in the mountains.

One

THE EARLY YEARS AND THE BUNCOMBE TURNPIKE

The first visitors to Asheville came on foot, through the mountains, on what was established in 1828 as the Buncombe Turnpike. Farmers drove their animals down the dirt path of the turnpike from Greeneville, Tennessee, to Greenville, South Carolina, and markets farther south. Traveling by foot through the rugged terrain of the Blue Ridge Mountains took time, and drovers needed a place to stay overnight where they could feed and water the hogs, cattle, horses, mules, turkeys, and ducks in their care. This annual migration included tens of thousands of animals and was a very lucrative business not only for the farmers, but also for the businessmen who opened up stands along the turnpike to cater to them.

The busiest months were October through December, when a stand could house a dozen drovers and anywhere from 300 to 2,000 animals. $1 would buy feed for the animals and a meal for the drover, who could sleep on the floor of the inn for free. Drovers often had to pay for their stays on their trip back through the mountains, once they had been paid at market in Greenville, Charleston, or even Atlanta. Alexander's Inn, later called Vance Hall, was the first drover's stand, or inn, in Asheville, and was soon followed by the Eagle and the Buck Hotel, both located on Main Street.

When the turnpike was not busy with hogs, stagecoaches ran along its beaten dirt path. The stagecoach line ran daily from Asheville to Greenville, from where travelers could then travel on to Charleston. Wealthy planters in the Lowcountry began to utilize this line, especially during the summer months, when the cool mountain climate offered them respite from the muggy air of the lowcountry summers.

In the early 1800s, Asheville had a population of only a few hundred people, but the stagecoach line allowed news, mail, household goods, and fashions from more populated areas to reach the still-remote area. The population reached 1,000 around 1851, when the turnpike was improved to offer easier, mud-free travel by way of a covering of thick wooden boards all the way to railroad-accessible Greenville, South Carolina.

VIEW AT ALEXANDERS.

Alexander's Inn, built by James Mitchel Alexander, was the first inn in Asheville. Situated between the Buncombe Turnpike and the east bank of the French Broad River, the inn provided for guests from its own dairy, gardens, and orchards, which comprised 162 acres of land. Guests could resupply at the general store, the shoe shop, the wagon factory, the gristmill, and the sawmill, and could use the river ferry that operated there as well. (Pack.)

Alexander's Inn hosted many well-known politicians, including John C. Calhoun, William C. Preston, and Pres. Andrew Johnson. The inn was said to offer a "true old-time Southern welcome." Alexander's was later sold to Robert Brank Vance, who renamed it Vance Hall. Vance had been a brigadier general in the Confederate army and a member of Congress for 12 years. (Pack.)

Built around 1814 by James Patton, the Eagle was recognizable to everyone by the gold eagle perched above the front door. Spanning the block between Eagle and Sycamore Streets on South Main Street (now Biltmore Avenue), the Eagle was originally built as a three-story frame construction, but was later converted to a brick structure. (Pack.)

James Patton also bought Warm Springs, named for its 100-plus-degree mineral water, in 1831. By 1837, he had built a grand hotel, nicknamed Patton's White House because of its size. The Warm Springs Hotel had 350 rooms and its dining room could seat 600. The original hotel burned down in 1884, and was replaced by Mountain Park Hotel, seen here, which burned down in 1920 and was not replaced. The area around it is now well known as Hot Springs. (Pack.)

A stagecoach ride from Asheville to Greeneville, Tennessee, about 60 miles, cost $1 and took a day. The coach would leave downtown at 5:30 a.m. and stop north of town at Alexander's Inn for breakfast. In the afternoon, another stop for dining would be made at Warm Springs, and the coach would reach Greeneville by evening. (Pack.)

The Eagle, seen here, was demolished in 1924 when Broadway was widened. (Pack.)

The Buck Hotel was located on North Main Street at what is now the corner of Broadway and College Street. It was built by James McConnell Smith. In the 1890s, around the time this photograph was taken, it became known as Mrs. Evan's boardinghouse. It was demolished in 1907, making room for a grander hotel, the Langren, to take its place. (Pack.)

With the revenue from his various business ventures, including the Buck Hotel, James Smith built himself a grand brick mansion just outside of Asheville. The Smith-McDowell House is the oldest surviving house in Asheville and the oldest brick house in Buncombe County. Smith married Polly Patton, the niece of James Patton, in 1814, the same year the Eagle was built. (Author.)

In the 1840s, there were less than 20 buildings in downtown Asheville, and nothing stood between the Buck Hotel and Woodfin Street. Drovers could keep their animals in the barn and swine yard, which was located where Pritchard Park is today. The animals were fed corn from James Smith's plantations, one of his many business ventures. He also had a general store, a tavern, a tannery, and a toll bridge. (Pack.)

Two

The Railroad Boom

The most important advance for tourism in Asheville was the connection of the railroad line to the rest of the country. A one-day trip in a stagecoach could only get patrons to Greeneville, Tennessee, about 60 miles away, while one day by rail could take patrons to New York City, 700 miles away.

The railroad came late to Asheville, about three decades after it reached most other Southern cities. This was initially due to the difficulty of getting through the mountains and was complicated further by the lack of funding for such a difficult project, especially in the aftermath of the Civil War. Although Asheville was less directly affected by the war than most Southern cities, it was not immune to the widespread poverty and general unrest that permeated the South after the war.

By the early 1880s, the railroad finally arrived in Asheville, bringing with it the need for upscale lodging. Tourists visiting from big cities were used to such luxuries as indoor plumbing, steam heat, and electric lights, and Asheville quickly accommodated them.

The Swannanoa, a massive three-story hotel on Main Street, upgraded to add the first bathroom in the city. In 1886, Col. Frank Coxe, vice president of the Western North Carolina Railroad Company, built a grand luxury hotel atop Asheville's largest hill, Battery Porter, which was used as a defense ramification during the Civil War. The Battery Park Inn was a huge rambling hotel with enormous porches that overlooked 1,000 square miles of scenic mountains. It also boasted the first electric lights and the first elevator in the area.

The Oakland Heights, Margo Terrace, and Kenilworth Inn were built soon after, as tourism boomed and the population of Asheville quadrupled from 2,600 to more than 10,000 between 1880 and 1890. Guests were entertained with carriage rides in the mountains, parlor games, musicales, and dancing.

In 1887, the first streetcar line was laid in Asheville, allowing visitors easy access from the passenger depot all the way to Pack Square. Electric lines also began to weave their way through the growing city.

The Swannanoa Hotel was built in 1880, two years before the railroad finally reached Asheville, at 65–75 Main Street (now Biltmore Avenue). It was soon upgraded with the addition of the first bathroom in western North Carolina, at the request of frequent guest George Pack. (Pack.)

This was the view from the upstairs balcony of the Swannanoa Hotel, looking up South Main Street towards the square. Stepping-stones provided a mud-free crosswalk across the street toward the Eagle Hotel, which is to the right of the barber pole. Streetcar, telephone, and electrical lines created complex webs above the horses and buggies in the streets. (Pack.)

MAIN STREET NORTH FROM SWANNANOA HOTEL—Asheville.

In 1887, Solomon Lipinsky opened a dry goods store in the bottom of the Swannanoa Hotel. He named it Bon Marché, or "good deal" in French, after the famous French department store Le Bon Marché in Paris. It eventually grew into one of the biggest and finest department stores in the state, and was a fixture in Asheville for more than 90 years. (Pack.)

Col. Frank Coxe, the vice president of the Western North Carolina Railroad, saw great potential in Asheville as a resort destination, and bought Battery Porter Hill to build a great hotel on it. Opening on July 26, 1886, the 150-room Battery Park Hotel was said to house 400 to 500 guests at rates of $2.50 to $3.50 per day. (Pack.)

The Battery Park Hotel was situated on Battery Porter Hill, or Stony Hill, as it was called before the Civil War. A 25-acre park of ancient oaks surrounded the hotel, and flower gardens were planted in what had been earthworks during the Civil War. At this time, Battery Porter Hill was the tallest peak in the city, 70 feet higher than it stands today. (Ball.)

As the first modern hotel in North Carolina, the Battery Park offered guests such amenities as 275 electric lamps, an Otis elevator, and steam heat. There was a newsstand and a telegraph office in the lobby and plenty of entertainment options, including billiards, a barroom, a shooting gallery, a bowling alley, smoking rooms, reading rooms, parlors, drawing rooms, ballrooms, and 475 feet of porches. (Author.)

The Battery Park offered guests access to its stables, which held 30–40 horses tended by 15–20 stable hands. Colonel Coxe enjoyed driving guests around the countryside and up Mount Pisgah or Mount Mitchell in Maude, his tallyho. George Vanderbilt hired horses from the stables while visiting the Battery Park and took them around what would eventually be his own 125,000-acre estate. (Pack.)

Presidents Theodore Roosevelt, Franklin Roosevelt, Grover Cleveland, and William McKinley (pictured here, at left in the backseat of the carriage) all visited the Battery Park. (Pack.)

In 1922, Edwin W. Grove bought the aging Battery Park Hotel with plans to take down the hotel and level the hill where it stood. Workers removed seven stories of dirt from Battery Hill and relocated it to a ravine near present-day Coxe Avenue, expanding building space for real estate in downtown Asheville. (Ball.)

As workers were busy with mules and steam shovels taking down the old Battery Park Hotel and removing 70 feet of hill, the hotel caught on fire. The blaze was left to burn out the last remnants of a great symbol of Victorian Asheville. (Ball.)

On the other side of town, visitors could find more affordable lodging at the Southern. Located at 26–28 South Main Street (now Biltmore Avenue), the Southern offered 26 large rooms for $1.50 a night and "dainty style" meals in the 25-seat dining room. This address later housed the Strauss European Hotel (1890), the Arcadia Hotel (1900), the Stoner European Hotel (1907), and the Paxton Hotel (1914). (Pack.)

In 1887, Alexander Garret became the mayor of the small town of Victoria, a fashionable neighborhood he founded just outside of Asheville. He lived with his family in what is now the Smith-McDowell House and built the Victoria Inn nearby in 1889. (Author.)

The Victoria Inn was a three-story frame building with 80 rooms and a 30,000-gallon water tower filled with "pure mountain water." On top of the tower was a circular room with 16 windows. (Pack.)

In 1896, the Victoria Inn became the Oakland Heights, which offered guests the services of Dr. Mary L. Edwards to treat nervous and chronic diseases. Advertisements reached out to "persons suffering from pressure of business and wearied by the cares and burdens of social life." (Pack.)

In 1909, after the town of Victoria was annexed into the city of Asheville, Oakland Heights once again became the Victoria Inn. The next year, the inn was converted to a Catholic day school named St. Genevieve of the Pines. This photograph was taken by Asheville photographer Herbert Pelton. (Pack.)

Built in 1889 by William Lewis Hunt, Margo Terrace was originally a 26-room boardinghouse. It was located on the corner of French Broad Avenue and Haywood Street on Battery Porter Hill. The stone wall seen in this photograph still exists as the base to a parking lot. (Pack Memorial Library, William A. Barnhill Collection.)

The Margo Terrace was described in newspaper ads as "the Leading Family Resort of Asheville. Reasonable Rates and Special Adaptability for Families and Ladies Traveling Alone." In 1904, it was enlarged to 64 rooms. It is seen here in the shadow of the new Battery Park Hotel (behind), built in 1924. The Margo Terrace was bought by Edwin W. Grove in 1925 and razed in 1928. (Pack.)

The Kenilworth Inn opened atop the second-highest peak in Asheville in 1890. After a five-minute ride from the depot to the inn, guests were guided under the impressive porte cochere and into the expansive lobby. The Kenilworth Inn grounds included 40 acres of lawn and 160 acres of wooded parkland. (Author.)

The Kenilworth Inn (shown in the distance) offered views of the recently acquired lands of George Vanderbilt, who, in the 1890s, was building his famous 250-room mansion, Biltmore House, just miles away. (Pack.)

In 1909, the Kenilworth Inn caught on fire. The fire, which started in the boiler room, completely destroyed the hotel, causing losses estimated at $250,000. (Pack.)

The *New York Times* reported that 75 guests fled the hotel in their nightclothes as the blaze caught and destroyed the grand hotel. It is described in the same article as being a fashionable place for northern tourists in the winter and a favorite meeting place for southern conventions in the summer. (D.H. Ramsey Library Special Collections, Holladay Collection of John B. Robinson Photographs.)

Asheville, N.C., Glen Rock Hotel.

Located directly across from the train depot, the Glen Rock Hotel capitalized on its convenient location. A three-story, wood-frame, Queen Anne–style hotel with a distinctive corner turret, the Glen Rock could accommodate 200 or more guests, catered to by 25–40 employees. The proprietor, A.G. Hallyburton, was said to have the finest cigars and whiskey. (Pack.)

All train passengers entered Asheville through the grand Southern Railway passenger station on Depot Street. A trolley ran from the depot up Livingston Street to downtown Asheville. After passenger train service to Asheville ended in the 1970s, the depot was demolished. (Pack.)

In 1916, a great flood hit Asheville, trapping guests inside the Glen Rock Hotel. Two men, Lonnie Trexler and Luther Frazer, died when they attempted to take food to the guests. The Glen Rock survived, but, 14 years later, it was condemned as a fire hazard and torn down. A new Glen Rock was put up in its place in the 1930s, and it still stands today on Depot Street. (Pack.)

At the southwest corner of Pack Square, the Western Hotel offered guests large, comfortable rooms and a neat, home-style dining room. One proprietor, Dr. L.B. McBrayer, graduated with high honors from Louisville Medical College in Kentucky and is described in the city directory as a "gentleman of push and vim [who] is bound to succeed in any enterprise he embarks in." (Pack.)

Three

THE TURN OF THE CENTURY

After the railroad boom of the 1880s, Asheville continued to grow. This was helped in part by George Vanderbilt's decision to build his palatial country estate, Biltmore, a few miles from downtown, adding to Asheville's reputation as a great destination city. The esteem that Vanderbilt and his fashionable wife, Edith, lent to the mountain town gave Northern city-dwellers reason to head down to North Carolina. From 1890 to 1910, the population nearly doubled again, from 10,235 to 18,762. In addition, 50,000 people visited Asheville on an annual basis. The most popular and easiest way to travel continued to be by rail, as roads through the mountains were less accommodating to early automobiles.

More grand hotels opened, including the Manor, on Charlotte Street, which provided cottages for families to rent that included servants' quarters, and the Langren, where the early Buck Hotel had once stood on North Main Street. Whereas the Manor catered to wealthy guests looking for a leisurely, extended stay, the Langren was built for a new kind of traveler: the businessman. While hotels had previously guarded themselves against traveling businessmen and conventions, opportunity began to be seen in this class of traveler, and Asheville openly catered to it. Guests during this period expected comfortable rooms, home-style meals, hot and cold water, and telephones.

Downtown Asheville was bustling with streetcars and businesses, including the Bon Marché department store, which first opened its doors on the bottom floor of the Swannanoa Hotel on Main Street and in 1911 took over the former Berkeley Hotel on Patton Avenue.

Residents and visitors in the early 1900s would find it hard to believe that today many people visit Asheville for its breweries, as Asheville was a dry city from 1908 until the repeal of Prohibition in 1933.

In 1898, the Manor opened on Charlotte Street. It was built as an English-style inn by railroad magnate William Greene Raoul and his son Thomas Wadley Raoul. Although the younger Raoul had originally come to Asheville to recuperate from tuberculosis, the Manor had strict policies banning those with the disease from staying at the inn. (Pack.)

In addition to the main building, the Manor also had 14 cottages that could house up to 12 guests each, as well as servants. (Author.)

The Manor strove to accommodate guests in a homelike environment, providing private cottages for rent and offering simple home-cooked meals as opposed to fancier fare. (Pack.)

None of the private cottages were built with kitchens, as all guests were expected to take their meals in the Manor's luxurious dining room. (Author.)

A promotional brochure for the Manor describes "quiet and efficient waitresses" and servants "on par." In 1928, the employees of the Manor published an open letter of thanks to the owner, Thomas W. Raoul. One of the signees was Susan Saxon, seen here, who worked there for over 19 years. (Pack.)

The fireplace inside of the sitting room was open on both sides, offering winter guests additional warmth to the steam heat used at the inn. (Pack.)

The large ballroom at the Manor was completed in 1903 and offered many social occasions for guests, including this New Year's Eve party in 1914. (Pack.)

In 1920, Thomas W. Raoul sold the Manor to Edwin W. Grove. It continued to operate as an inn, under various owners, until 1990. (D.H. Ramsey Library Special Collections, Holladay Collection of John B. Robinson Photographs.)

Built in 1856 as a dormitory for the Asheville Female College, the building was sold in 1887 and became the Oaks Hotel, and the Cherokee Inn in 1908. In 1920, it was purchased by the YWCA, and was demolished before 1927 and replaced by the Douglas Ellington–designed First Baptist Church. (Pack.)

The Oaks Hotel offered rooms for the traveling public and for health and pleasure seekers. The 100 guest rooms had gas, electric bells, and hot and cold baths. Streetcars passed the hotel every 10 minutes, and a large telescope 80 feet above the ground offered views of the city and the mountains. (Pack.)

Located at 21–23 Patton Avenue, on the site of what is now the Kress Building, the Berkeley Hotel closed in 1911 to merge with the Swannanoa Hotel on Biltmore Avenue. (Pack.)

Situated just a block from the town square, the Swannanoa-Berkeley Hotel continued to enjoy popularity through the early 1900s. It advertised comfortable rooms, hot and cold water, long-distance telephone service, and a large ballroom where many social functions were held. (Ball.)

Solomon Lipinsky moved his Bon Marché department store to the site of the former Berkeley Hotel on Patton Avenue and kept it there until 1923. In 1938, Thomas Wolfe wrote Lewis Lipinsky, Solomon's son, "Bon Marché is such a landmark in Asheville life that if I ever heard anything had happened to it I think I should feel almost as if Beaucatcher Mountain had been violently removed from the landscape by some force of nature." (Pack.)

The new Bon Marché location on Patton Avenue is seen here on the left during a 1920s parade. The Louisiana Hotel, across the street, was on the corner of Patton and Lexington Avenues. The Vance Monument is visible in the distance. (Pack.)

The Langren was built on the site of the previous Buck Hotel, at College Street and Biltmore Avenue. Construction began in 1908, but, soon after the framework was done, the builder ran into money problems, and it remained an unfinished shell until it was bought by Gay Green and John H. Lange, whom the hotel was named after. (Pack.)

When it opened for business on July 4, 1912, the Langren was one of the biggest hotels in the region. Unlike the Battery Park Hotel, the Langren catered mostly to businessmen. A room cost around $1 per night, or $3 for a corner room. (Author.)

The day after the Langren opened, the General Passenger Department of the Southern Railway visited the hotel. In the center of the photograph, seated in a light suit and holding a hat, is one

of the owners of the Langren, John Lange. The mayor of Asheville, J.E. Rankin, is immediately to the left of him. (Pack.)

Gay Green and John Lange operated the hotel until 1933, when it was leased out. (Pack.)

If this photograph, which dates to 1936–1941, had been taken 100 years earlier, downtown Asheville would have looked much different. The Buck Hotel would have stood where the Langren is here, in the left background, and hogs and cattle belonging to drovers would have been grazing in what became Pritchard Park, in the left foreground. (Pack.)

The 1921 silent film *Conquest of Canaan* was one of the first and most popular movies shot in Asheville. The old Swannanoa-Berkeley Hotel was renamed the Canaan City Hotel for the film, and the Langren Hotel (right) was the backdrop for this shot in Pack Square. (Ball.)

In 1918, Asheville celebrated the end of World War I with a parade and celebration in and around Pack Square. (Ball.)

The Langren was in the middle of the World War I victory celebration. During this time, the hotel had a soldiers' club for enlisted men on the bottom level. (Ball.)

In 1964, the Langren was bought by Northwestern Bank, which razed it and built a parking garage on the site. It is now the BB&T parking garage. (Ball.)

Four

RENTAL VILLAS, BOARDINGHOUSES, AND SANITARIUMS

Large, fashionable inns were not the only places to stay in Asheville in the early 1900s. Very wealthy guests could choose the bigger, more private option of a rental villa. George Vanderbilt built a total of six such villas that were designed by Richard Sharp Smith, the supervising architect of the Biltmore Estate. These 2.5-story pebble-dash villas rented for between $200 and $350 per month, while hotels would run between $30 and $180 for the same length of time.

People looking for a cheaper, cozier option could find lodging at one of the dozens of boardinghouses in Asheville. Early in the century, the *New York Times* quoted from an Asheville guidebook, stating, "Nearly everyone keeps boarders." The 1915 *Asheville Directory* lists 102 entries under boardinghouses, and many that were in operation may have not have been listed. The town, which had a population of about 19,000 in 1910, was estimated to have room for 12,000–15,000 guests in its boardinghouses, only charging between $24 and $56 per month.

The reputed curative powers of the mountain air attracted numerous patients with tuberculosis and other lung ailments. In the late 1800s and early 1900s, tuberculosis was one of the most deadly diseases in the country, and since prevention and treatment were not fully understood, it was greatly feared. To meet the demands of patients while keeping the regular tourist lodgings disease-free, sanitariums began to open up throughout the city. The first tuberculosis sanitarium in the United States, called simply the Villa, was opened in Asheville by Dr. H.P. Gatchell in 1871.

Other famous doctors followed Dr. Gatchell, including Dr. Joseph Gleitsmann, Dr. Karl Von Ruck, and Dr. S. Westray Battle, who treated George Vanderbilt's mother, Maria, as well as Edwin W. Grove, who suffered from long bouts of hiccups. Ironically, when Grove began building the Grove Park Inn 15 years after first coming to Asheville, he became concerned that the sanitariums would drive away tourists, so he bought a number of them and burned them down. When antibiotics were developed to treat tuberculosis, the need for sanitariums dwindled. At its peak, Asheville had 25 sanitariums, but the last had closed by the end of the 1950s.

Designed by Richard Sharpe Smith, the supervising architect of the Biltmore Estate and many other buildings around Asheville, Sunnicrest is the only surviving of the six villas built for George Vanderbilt. They were available as fully furnished rental mansions on Vernon Hill in the fashionable town of Victoria, which was later annexed into Asheville. (Author.)

Built in 1900, Spurwood, like Vanderbilt's other rental villas, rented for between $200 and $350 per month. The rental included everything except linen, silver, and blankets. In 1911, the *New York Times* announced the sale of two of George Vanderbilt's rental villas. Spurwood sold for $20,000. (Pack.)

Raised in his mother's boardinghouse, My Old Kentucky Home, Thomas Wolfe wrote about Asheville in his most famous novel, *Look Homeward, Angel*, thinly veiling his fiction with name changes such as Dixieland for the boardinghouse on Woodfin Street. In the 1910s and 1920s, Julia Wolfe charged $7–$10 per week for a room and three meals a day. (Pack Memorial Library, Thomas Wolfe Collection.)

Today, the Thomas Wolfe House is open for tours and offers visitors a glimpse of life in Asheville in the early 1900s. (Author.)

The Brexler boardinghouse, at 33 Starnes Avenue, was opened in 1895 and run independently by women until 1906, when St. Joseph's Hospital Sisters of Mercy added sleeping porches and opened it as a sanitarium for tuberculosis patients. In 1910, it returned to the tourist trade and was renamed the Willard. (Author.)

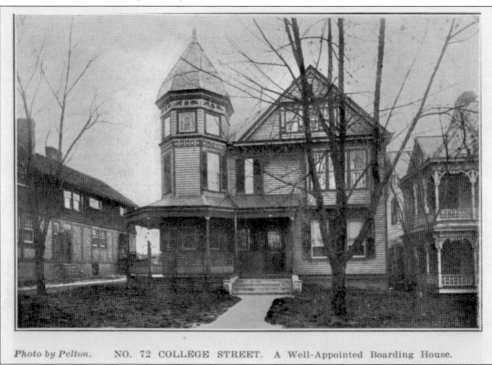

Photo by Pelton.   NO. 72 COLLEGE STREET.   A Well-Appointed Boarding House.

Located at 72 College Street, Chatham boardinghouse was "well-appointed," according to the *Souvenir Directory to the Land of the Sky*, published in Waynesville in 1910. (Pack.)

A "Commodius Gothic Mansion," according to the 1912 Asheville city directory, Ridgelawn was remodeled and refurbished and sat on several acres of well-shaded lawn appointed with hammocks and swings for guests' enjoyment. (Pack.)

When Dr. Karl Von Ruck opened Winyah in 1888, it was the only sanitarium in Asheville besides the Villa, which was the first sanitarium in the country when it was opened by Dr. H.P. Gatchell in 1871. Other tuberculosis patients visiting Asheville and looking for a cure stayed at boardinghouses with porches. By 1930, there were 25 sanitariums in Asheville, with around 900 total beds for patients. (Pack.)

Dr. Robert S. Carroll was a psychiatrist who specialized in mental and nervous disorders and addictions. He opened Dr. Carroll's Sanitarium downtown in 1904, relocated it to the north end of Montford Avenue in 1909, and renamed it Highland Hospital in 1912. His patients were treated through exercise, diet, and occupational therapy. (Pack.)

In 1936, writer F. Scott Fitzgerald admitted his wife, Zelda, to Highland Hospital to be treated for schizophrenia. She spent the remainder of her life in and out of Highland. On March 10, 1948, a fire broke out in the central building of the hospital, killing Zelda and eight other women. (Pack.)

In 1912, Dr. William Banks Meacham opened the 18-room Ottari Sanitarium on Kimberly Avenue. Filled with Persian rugs, silk draperies, mahogany furniture, suites with private porches, and a fish aquarium, it was advertised as the "finest private sanitarium ever built." It more than doubled in size in 1923, when 23 new rooms were added. The building currently houses the Coburn Apartments. (Author.)

Located on Black Mountain State Highway four miles outside of Asheville, Ambler Heights Sanitarium was opened by Chase P. Ambler and his son Arthur C. Ambler to offer the best tuberculosis care in the area. Before opening his own medical practice, Chase Ambler had worked at Winyah Sanitarium in Asheville under Dr. Karl Von Ruck. (Pack.)

Today, Chase P. Ambler is best known in Asheville for the ruins of his hunting cabin, Rattlesnake Lodge, a popular hiking destination north of the city off the Blue Ridge Parkway. He is also credited with initiating the idea of creating a national park in the southern Appalachian Mountains, which eventually evolved into the dedication of Great Smoky Mountains National Park on April 22, 1926. (Pack.)

All the rooms at Ambler Heights had sleeping porches and steam-heated dressing rooms. Doctors at the time felt that the clean, cool mountain air was the most important prescription for the cure of tuberculosis. (Pack.)

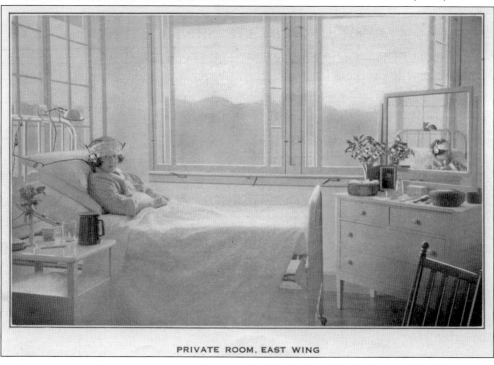

PRIVATE ROOM, EAST WING

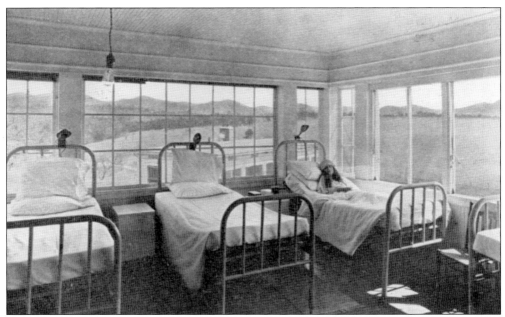

Although it advertised that advanced cases should be accommodated elsewhere, Ambler Heights Sanitarium continued to treat tuberculosis patients until the 1920s. (Pack.)

The Princess Anne Hotel, at 301 East Chestnut Street, was built in 1924 by registered nurse Anne O'Connell and financed by Dr. Karl Von Ruck of the Winyah Sanitarium. The hotel catered to the families of patients being treated nearby at O'Connell's Sanitarium on Baird Street. (Ball.)

Nurse Anne O'Connell was often called "Princess" because of her beauty, her lovely red hair, and her charming nature; therefore, her hotel was called the Princess Anne. O'Connell ran the hotel through 1929 and promised "comfort first" for all her guests. (Pack.)

Like many historic hotels in Asheville, the Princess Anne has changed hands and purposes multiple times through the years. The hotel was once owned by George Anderson Mercer, the father of the famous songwriter Johnny Mercer. It was then used by Appalachian Hall, a psychiatric hospital that also took over the Kenilworth Inn. From 1957 to 1995, it functioned as a retirement home. In 2003, it was bought, renovated, and returned to its former glory as a hotel. (Pack.)

Five

THE GROVE PARK INN

The Grove Park Inn is by far the most iconic inn in Asheville. As secretary of state William Jennings Bryan said on opening night, the Grove Park Inn was "built for the ages." Edwin Wiley Grove, a self-made millionaire from Tennessee, began spending summers in Asheville on the advice of his doctors, who were treating him for his constant bouts of hiccups. Grove had made his fortune as the founder of the St. Louis–based Paris Medicine Company, and he was always looking for new business ventures. He soon realized the need for a large luxury inn to house the whole host of visitors coming to Asheville on a yearly basis.

After issuing an open call for designs, he found what he was looking for in a sketch by Fred Seely, a young partner in the Paris Medicine Company and Grove's son-in-law. With no previous experience in architecture, Seely had drawn the sketch that Grove had been looking for, based roughly on Yellowstone's Old Faithful Inn and using native boulders to blend it into the mountain scenery. After approving the plan, Grove and Seely walked the land Grove owned at the base of Sunset Mountain to pinpoint the perfect location for the inn. On July 9, 1912, Grove's second wife, Gertrude, turned the first shovel of dirt at the ground-breaking.

In and out of fashion, remodeled, updated, and finally returned to its roots; 100 years later, the Grove Park Inn still sits nestled into Sunset Mountain. It represents what happens when people with multiple talents come together: those with the ideas to envision and the money to fund, those with the strength to stack boulders, and those with the land to build on. Grove came up with the idea and the money, and Seely brought the idea to life. But it could not have been truly great without those working behind the scenes, in their denim overalls or crisp aprons and rubber-heeled shoes, laying both the heavy stones and the soft linens.

Edwin W. Grove came to Asheville on the advice of his doctors because he was looking for a cure for his prolonged hiccups. He had made a fortune in the pharmaceutical business developing Grove's Tasteless Chill Tonic, a treatment for malaria, which was a deadly disease in the southern United States in the early 1900s. (GPI.)

While meeting with Edwin W. Grove about business ventures, Fred Loring Seely fell in love with Grove's daughter Evelyn. This meeting was beneficial for all, as Seely ended up being the chief architect of the Grove Park Inn. Here, Seely drives the lead car on a tour of mountain roads. Seely also left his mark on Asheville with his famous Overlook Castle on Town Mountain Road. (Pack.)

Local farmers got to work loading rocks from the mountain even before the first dirt was shoveled for the inn. Hundreds of mules pulled wagons and sleds full of rocks and boulders to a waiting automobile train. Pulleys and ropes helped move the stones, some weighing as much as 10,000 pounds, from Sunset, Beaucatcher, and Black Mountains. (GPI.)

The "automobile train" was a Packard truck that pulled 15 wagons holding more than 40 tons of rocks down the mountain. (GPI.)

The scaffolding used in building the inn likely came from Grove's sawmill and lumberyard in Madison County. (GPI.)

Fred Seely explained his specific instructions for the boulders: "Not a piece of stone should be visible to the eye except it show the time-eaten face given to it by the thousands of years of sun and rain that had beaten upon it as it had lain on the mountain side. These great boulders were laid with the lichens and moss on them just as they were found." (GPI.)

The two fireplaces in the great hall are 36 feet wide and were built with 120 tons of boulders each. They are large enough to burn eight-foot logs held in place by hammered-iron andirons that weigh 500 pounds apiece. (GPI.)

This photograph is dated just two days before the formal opening of the inn, on July 12, 1913. Although Edwin Grove was wary of the hurried timetable, Seely vowed to finish the inn within a year. In the end, he was just three days over schedule. (GPI.)

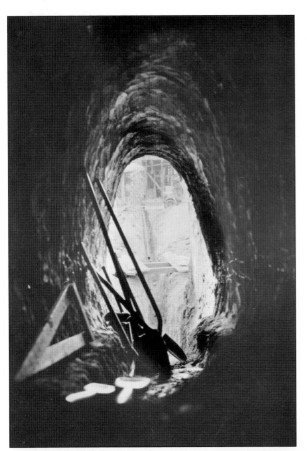

Although this tunnel was probably for water pipes, today, stone-lined tunnels lead underground to the world-famous Grove Park Inn spa. (GPI.)

The original first-floor stairs, located across from the elevators, were later removed. Seely placed the elevators themselves inside the back of the fireplace in order to muffle any noise the mechanics made. (GPI.)

58

A total of 400 men of various ages and races were hired to build the Grove Park Inn. The pay was the best in the area: $1 a day for a 10-hour shift. Workers traveled from nearby and farther south, abandoning other projects for the opportunity to work on the inn. A circus tent was erected on the grounds to house the workers. (GPI.)

Fred Seely commissioned the Roycrofters to furnish 400 straight-backed oak chairs for the inn that bore a prominent "GPI," along with the identifying Roycroft orb-and-cross as seen here emblazoned on the front of the chair. The majority of these chairs were sold off in 1955 for $5 apiece, although about 20 remain in the inn's collection. (GPI.)

This photograph, taken by Herbert Pelton on November 2, 1912, is captioned, "The men who

are building the Grove Park Inn." (GPI.)

Dozens of mules and horses were also used to move not only the mountain itself, but also all of the supplies needed to put it back together into the shape of an inn. (GPI.)

Only one piece of motorized equipment, the steam shovel, was used to build the Grove Park Inn. The rest of the work was done the old-fashioned way—by hand. The shovel helped workers carve the ledge that the inn would rest on into the mountain. (GPI.)

Coal was used to power the complicated system of chains and pulleys of the steam shovel, which had only been produced on a large scale in the United States for a few decades when this photograph was taken. The speed and strength of the new machine revolutionized building practices. (GPI.)

The Grove Park Inn was touted in advertisements as "Absolutely Fireproof." The granite walls on some parts of the inn are four feet thick. (GPI.)

Here, workers finish the base of the roof before adding the famous red clay tiles. (GPI.)

Timber provided a building foundation for the boulders and was also used as scaffolding. This photograph shows the precarious walkway built for the workers to push a heavy wheelbarrow full of cement up to the roof, 80 feet above. (GPI.)

The granite walls and concrete floors that made the inn fireproof caused endless problems in later decades when water and electrical lines had to be replaced. (GPI.)

This interior view, taken three months before the opening of the inn, shows the wooden foundation of the walls and ceiling as well as stacks of windows waiting to be installed. (GPI.)

A total of 15 carloads of fireproof red clay tiles were shipped in from Kentucky for the Grove Park Inn. The tiles are seen here still in their packaging, waiting for the roof to be ready. These tiles were nailed to the fireproof roof cement with 1.5 tons of coppered-steel nails. (GPI.)

Workers often stayed through the night, necessitating the installation of large lights to aid their tireless work. In this photograph, the safety lines attaching them to the roof, 80 feet off the ground, can be seen as workers weave the steel rods over the initial wood form. (GPI.)

Five inches of cement were reinforced with 90,000 pounds of steel rods. On top of the rebar, five layers of hot tar were inlaid with three layers of asbestos felt. In order to attach the tens of thousands of red clay tiles, another layer of concrete was poured and laid with long, narrow wooden boards for the tiles to be nailed into. (GPI.)

The concrete roof was poured continuously to avoid seams. To do this, workmen pushed wheelbarrows of wet cement to an elevator that took them 80 feet up to the top of the roof, where they crossed a narrow walkway to other workers waiting with rakes and shovels to spread the concrete into an even layer across the roof. (GPI.)

The Grove Park Inn was originally comprised of five parts laid end to end, and offered guests 156 rooms. The red clay roof remains the most distinctive feature of the hotel, with the soft curves blending beautifully with the mountain surrounding the inn. The original roof, built with great care and no help from machinery, lasted for more than 90 years before having to be replaced. (GPI.)

The Palm Court allowed all rooms to have outside views and also provided natural air-conditioning. By opening the skylight in the roof above the sixth floor, hot air was pulled out of guest rooms through transoms above doors and then out the skylight, while fresh mountain air was pulled in through open windows. (GPI.)

This May 1913 photograph shows work on the 500 feet of terraces the inn would eventually boast. (GPI.)

Workers are seen here towards the end of May 1913. Discarded timbers litter the hillside where stairs would eventually lead down towards the 18-hole golf course of the Asheville Country Club. Many workers are posed climbing up the boulders of the inn, obviously comfortable with their workmanship. (GPI.)

Workers lay the original gray tile floor in the dining room. The same tile was used in the great hall and covered with rugs made in Aubusson, France. (GPI.)

In order to finish the inn by his scheduled opening date of July 12, 1913, Fred Seely had to pool his resources and leave certain parts of the inn unfinished, including the guest rooms of the sixth floor, the indoor swimming pool, and the landscaping. (Pack Memorial Library, William A. Barnhill Collection.)

The inn was formally opened on July 12, 1913, to an all-male dinner of 400 guests. Fred Loring Seely served as the toastmaster, and secretary of state William Jennings Bryan gave a speech in which he stated the inn was "built for the ages." (GPI.)

This advertisement from 1913, the year the Grove Park Inn opened, offers rooms for $7 a day and upward. Another advertisement from the same year warns, "Persons with any form of tubercular trouble will not be received at the Inn." (Ball.)

An early brochure written by Fred Seely states that there is "probably no place in the world where the climate is finer in the summer and the fall than in Asheville." This postcard shows that this was true in the spring as well. While most local resorts closed in the slow winter months, the Grove Park Inn was open year-round. (Author.)

Plantation Room--Grove Park Inn, Asheville, N. C.

The menus were fully explained, with the idea that people who could afford to stay at the inn were busy and needed good food and easy digestion. Long before local food became a trend, the Grove Park Inn advertised the exclusive use of Biltmore dairy products. (Pack.)

A total of 500 feet of terraces stretched around the inn, bedecked with rocking chairs for guests to enjoy. (GPI.)

The front lawn of the Grove Park Inn was the 120-acre Donald Ross–designed Asheville Country Club golf course, which guests could play. Those who did not golf could enjoy the other 60 acres of lawn and the 1,000 acres of woods the inn owned on Sunset Mountain. (GPI.)

The Heywood Brothers & Wakefield Company provided the wicker furniture for the great hall, including the famous rockers with red-leather seat cushions that occupied popular real estate in front of the large fireplaces. They were replaced in the 1930s when new management took over from Fred Seely. (Pack.)

Women were asked not to smoke in the great hall. A 1922 brochure elaborates: "We do not make this request with any inclination to be critical. It is simply a rule that has been observed ever since the inn was built and we believe that it conforms to the feelings of the majority of our household." (GPI.)

LOBBY, GROVE PARK INN - ASHEVILLE, N.C.

The "big room," as the great hall was once called, is 120 feet long and 80 feet wide—large enough to accommodate 1,000 people. The large Roycroft chandeliers were altered to allow more light in the 1930s renovation, and the wicker furniture was replaced by paddle-armed seats made by Old Hickory Furniture. (Pack.)

Elbert Hubbard, the founder of the Roycroft community of craftsmen in East Aurora, New York, would enclose slips of paper typed with inspirational mottos into his correspondence with friends and clients. While doing business with Hubbard, Fred Seely was inspired to include some of these mottoes throughout the inn on rocks, clocks, and furniture such as this screen. Many of these can still be seen today. (GPI.)

Located above the ceiling of the great hall and accessible by taking one of the elevators built behind the fireplace, the Palm Court provides a second lobby for guests on the third floor. Filled with palms and topped with a glass skylight, the Palm Court provides an airy escape. (Pack.)

An indoor swimming pool (below) in the recreation room was available to early guests of the Grove Park, although it was not finished until after the inn officially opened its doors. In 1928, new owners remodeled the inn to make it more attractive for businessmen and corporate conventions, turning many parlors and the recreation areas on the lower level, including the pool and the three-lane bowling alley, into meeting spaces. (GPI.)

Fred Seely had envisioned the Grove Park Inn as a big home with modern conveniences "but with all the old-fashioned qualities of genuineness with no sham." In addition to providing furniture for the dining room and other first-floor rooms, Roycroft Furniture Shop also provided the inn with 2,500 hammered-copper drawer pulls for dressers and desks, as well as the lighting for the guest rooms. (GPI.)

The furniture for the guest rooms was made by the White Furniture Company of North Carolina. It was based on models that Roycroft had sent to Fred Seely and fitted with hammered-copper pulls made by Roycroft. The simple Arts and Crafts style was accentuated by Roycroft copper light fixtures and lamps, as well as burlap wall coverings. (GPI.)

Under Seely's management, the inn maintained a rule of quiet. Guests that were being too loud in the great hall were handed a note to quiet down. A sign in the elevator asked guests to "Please be quiet in going to your room . . . we greatly desire quiet in the bedrooms and corridors from 10:30pm until 8am." (GPI.)

No automobiles were permitted to enter the grounds after 10:30 p.m. or before 9:00 a.m., so as not to interrupt guests resting. (GPI.)

Waiters were dressed in crisp white suits with sleeves that buttoned tightly around the wrists. They were lectured daily and continually checked for appearance. All employees wore rubber-heeled shoes to muffle their footsteps, and they were not permitted to clean or make noise before 9:00 a.m. At one point, Seely even instructed employees to cut water to guest rooms after 10:30 p.m. to aid in his pursuit of absolute quiet. (GPI.)

Children and pets were not permitted at the Grove Park Inn. One advertisement states, "Not that we dislike children, but that we wish to maintain a place where tired busy people may get away from excitement and all annoyances and rest their nerves." People smuggling in dogs of any "size, value, color or ugliness" were asked to vacate the inn. (Pack.)

In 1944, along with other major Asheville hotels, the Grove Park Inn was used by the US military to give brief respite to returning World War II servicemen and women. (Pack.)

In 1918, Harvey Firestone (partially obscured at far left), Thomas Edison (second from left), Harvey Firestone Jr. (third from left), Henry Ford (second from right), and Fred Seely (far right) visited the Grove Park Inn during a camping trip. Crowds of people awaited their arrival and greeted them from Mars Hill College all the way to the Grove Park Inn, where they feasted until midnight in the dining room after greeting reporters and guests in the great hall. (Pack.)

The Grove Park Inn has been a favorite wedding and honeymoon destination since it opened. (GPI.)

Deer were kept at the inn for guests' enjoyment. Opossums were also kept for possum stew, a favorite of secretary of state William Jennings Bryan. (Pack.)

A short car ride could take guests to go swimming at Beaver Lake, dancing in downtown Asheville, or to a movie at Riverside Park. (Pack.)

In 1955, new owners modernized the Grove Park Inn, plastering over the columns in the great hall, replacing the iconic rockers and Roycroft dining room chairs, and painting the plantation room turquoise and olive. In 1956, a more "modern" cloverleaf heated swimming pool was opened outside the west veranda, but it was demolished in the early 1980s. (Pack.)

Sunset Hall was built in 1913. It served as a servants' hall and employee residence. (Pack.)

In 1990, Sunset Hall was demolished to make way for the current sports complex (Ball.)

In 1901, the Vanderbilts created Biltmore Industries to train young people to make handmade crafts. Three years after George Vanderbilt passed away, his wife, Edith, sold the operations to Fred Seely, who moved Biltmore Industries to new outbuildings on the Grove Park Inn campus. The fine wool cloth they were famous for is still being made at the 1917 site using the original procedures and equipment. (Ball.)

The stables were turned into an automobile garage in 1924 and a gas station served hotel vehicles nearby. Both buildings were later razed. (Ball.)

The Grove Park Inn fell on hard times from 1932 to 1955. Charles Sammons, the owner of Jack Tar Hotels, bought the inn in 1955 for $400,000 and attempted to resuscitate business by modernizing it. (Pack.)

After 1908, the sale of liquor was illegal in Asheville. However, thirsty guests bypassed local laws by bringing their own stock to the inn and having it served to them by the Grove Park Inn waiters. It was not until the repeal of Prohibition in 1933 that the inn was able to facilitate the legal sale of alcohol. The first cocktail lounge, the Francis Marion Room, was opened in 1935. (Pack.)

In an effort to revive the Grove Park Inn in 1958, a motor lodge known as the Fairway Lodge was added at a cost of $200,000. The lodge, seen here to the right of the main inn, was torn down in 1982 to make way for a $20 million 202-room addition, the Sammons Wing. The Vanderbilt Wing was built on the opposite side in 1988. (Pack.)

In 1978, the Grove Park Inn was de-modernized, after which business returned. With the addition of the Sammons and Vanderbilt wings onto the hotel in the 1980s, the inn now has a total of 510 guest rooms. After a century of different owners and multiple renovations, one can still feel the same rustic, welcoming charm when seated in front of the crackling fireplace of the great hall. (Author.)

Six

THE ROARING TWENTIES

The years after World War I were vibrant in Asheville. The city remained a fashionable resort town, and more hotels were built to accommodate the visitors arriving by train and automobile.

In 1899, the Good Roads Association of Asheville and Buncombe County formed a campaign for government highway development. The organization was led by Dr. Chase P. Ambler, owner of Ambler Heights Sanitarium. By 1912, the accomplishments of the Good Roads Association had made Asheville accessible from Knoxville, Charlotte, and Greenville, South Carolina, as well as from a scenic mountain road along the Blue Ridge Mountains. These roads helped to bring new prosperity and tourists to Asheville.

In the 1920s, rates at one of the major Asheville hotels such as the new Battery Park Hotel or the Grove Park Inn went from $2.50 per day all the way to $10 per day. Boardinghouses were still popular at this time, and were offered from $15 to $25 a week. By 1929, the city directory listed 28 hotels and an annual influx of 250,000 visitors. The city was growing and real estate was being readily snatched up as the population almost doubled between 1920 and 1930, going from 28,504 to 50,193.

Edwin W. Grove capitalized on the real estate boom by purchasing the 30-year-old Battery Park Hotel and then tearing it down and leveling the hill it sat on to create more buildable land in downtown Asheville. In its place, he built a new Battery Park Hotel and the Grove Arcade, an indoor shopping area that was the largest building in this section of the country. Another hotel, the George Vanderbilt, was built across the street by local businessmen. Asheville's first skyscraper, the Jackson Building, was built where Thomas Wolfe's father once had a small monument shop.

Thanks to advances in medicine, the tuberculosis sanitariums faded away, but businessmen, conventions, honeymooning couples, wealthy northerners, and southern families were all taking the train or the new mountain roads to Asheville. The city streets, lined with shops, restaurants, and inns, were often filled with trolleys and parades.

By the 1920s, while the train was still a quite popular way to travel, automobiles were becoming popular as well, as evidenced by this 1924 photograph by George Masa. The new Battery Park Hotel is seen the center, with Margo Terrace on the left and the Basilica of St. Lawrence on the right. (Pack.)

In 1913, James Chiles began building a new Kenilworth Inn, a huge resort able to house 500 guests, on the site of the previous Kenilworth, which had been completely destroyed by a fire. (Ball.)

U.S.A. General Hospital No.12, Biltmore, N.C.
Main Hospital Building (Kenilworth Inn)
Showing enclosed Porches.

80-150

Before the new Kenilworth Inn opened, the US Army took over the building, making it US General Hospital No. 12 and using it from 1917 to 1922. A group of 180 German prisoners housed in nearby Hot Springs was moved to the hospital after the men contracted typhoid fever. The 18 prisoners who died during their stay are buried at Riverside Cemetery in Asheville. (Ball.)

In 1923, the Kenilworth Inn finally reopened. Guests were met with modern amenities and gorgeous views of the mountains. The entertainment options were varied, including tennis, golf, dancing, horseback riding, billiards, and picnics on the front lawn. The escape artist Harry Houdini even beguiled guests once at the Kenilworth. (Ball.)

The owner of the Kenilworth Inn, James Chiles, was also the mayor of Kenilworth. When he died, his wife, Leah, became the first female mayor in the state of North Carolina. (Ball.)

The Kenilworth Inn was built with multiple terraces and verandas so visitors could take in the healthy mountain air and enjoy the spectacular views. (Author.)

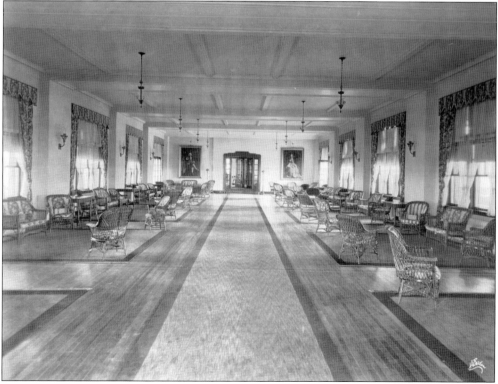

The Kenilworth Inn strove to be a major part of the social scene in Asheville. It advertised for the public to visit "any day or night of the week for dance, music and family fun." (Pack.)

Anyone living within 1,500 miles of the Kenilworth Inn could listen to the orchestra play from the music hall, as their performances were transmitted over the radio station WFAJ from the inn. (Pack.)

Mrs. John Francis Amherst Cecil (the former Cornelia Vanderbilt) and her husband were sponsors of the Kenilworth Galleries, which hosted artists from around the country and the world at the inn. She is seen here on the left, with Katherine Clark Pendleton Arrington, president of the Carolina State Art Society. (Pack.)

In 1928, the Kenilworth art show was the largest showcase of paintings in the South. More than 100 artists from 12 states and 3 foreign countries, including noted German and Italian painters, were exhibited at the Kenilworth Inn. (Pack.)

The art show continued yearly until 1930, when the Kenilworth Inn was sold and became Appalachian Hall, a private psychiatric hospital. (Pack.)

In June 1926, the Kenilworth Inn welcomed 200 florists from eight states with a banquet, a ball,

and an afternoon tea and organ recital at the Grove Park Inn, hosted by Fred Seely. (Pack.)

The Kenilworth Inn was negatively affected by the Depression and the annexation of Kenilworth into Asheville. It closed in 1930, and the building was then used by Appalachian Hall, a psychiatric hospital. The Kenilworth Inn still stands high above Asheville. Today, as with the Manor, it is rented out as apartments. (Author.)

In 1923, a group of Asheville businessmen, the Citizens Hotel Corporation, opened a 200-room luxury hotel at 75 Haywood Street that cost nearly $1 million to build. A newspaper contest was held to select a name for the hotel, the George Vanderbilt. (Ball.)

The architect of the George Vanderbilt Hotel, William Lee Stoddard, also designed the new Battery Park Hotel and the Bon Marché Building, at the corner of Haywood Street and Battery Park Avenue. (Author.)

Before the George Vanderbilt closed as a hotel in 1966, it hosted many visitors, including Richard Nixon, who stayed there on June 5, 1957, when he was vice president. (Pack.)

The Asheville City Auditorium (above, left) was built in 1940 for $247,000. It replaced a previous 1904 auditorium. The current civic center opened after much debate in 1974. (Pack.)

Today, the former George Vanderbilt Hotel operates as the Vanderbilt Apartments, a senior living facility in the heart of downtown Asheville. (Author.)

Downtown Asheville is seen here around 1924 from Beaucatcher Mountain. Both the new Battery Park Hotel and the George Vanderbilt Hotel are under construction just right of the center. Also under construction is the Jackson Building, just left of the center, which was completed that same year. (Ball.)

The last mound of dirt is removed by steam shovel and truck and taken to fill in a ravine to create Coxe Avenue. A portion of the porch of the new Battery Park Hotel is visible in the lower left corner. (Ball.)

Thomas Wolfe describes the new Battery Park Hotel as "being stamped out of the same mold, as if by some gigantic biscuit-cutter of hotels that had produced a thousand others like it all over the country." This holds some truth, as the same architect, William Lee Stoddard, also designed the George Vanderbilt Hotel and dozens of other urban hotels throughout the United States. (Ball.)

The 220-room, 14-story Battery Park Hotel was completed in 1924. The Grove Arcade would later occupy the square plot of land directly in front of it. Margo Terrace is on the left, although it was not there for long after this photograph was taken. (Pack.)

The foundation for the Grove Arcade, seen here in the foreground, was laid in 1926. Edwin W. Grove passed away in 1927 before it could be finished, and his dream of a 14-story tower topping the building was cut short. (Ball.)

The Grove Arcade was completed in 1929. It was filled with shops and fulfilled Grove's vision of providing customers with a place to park and shop without running to different areas of town. It is considered one of the country's first indoor shopping malls. (Ball.)

This photograph of the interior of the new Battery Park Hotel shows that it was just as luxurious as its Victorian predecessor. (Pack.)

The new Battery Park Hotel was the center of a vibrant social scene for tourists and locals alike. Balls, concerts, bridge tournaments, teas, and conferences were all held there. This view of the ballroom makes it obvious why. (Pack.)

The WLOS radio station operated out of the southeast corner of the Battery Park Hotel from 1947 to 1954. (Ball.)

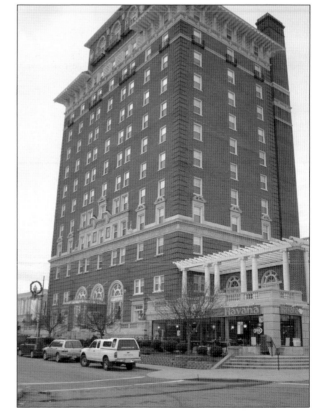

The Battery Park operated as a hotel until 1972. In the 1980s, the Asheville Housing Authority converted it into housing for seniors, similar to the facility that took over the George Vanderbilt Hotel. (Author.)

Previously the Southern, and, before that, multiple other hotels, the Albirt Hotel (above, right) was located at 26–28 South Main Street (now Biltmore Avenue). The Langren Hotel is seen in the background of this photograph, and Finkelstein's Pawn Shop, "North Carolina's Oldest Pawnbroker," is on the left, at 23–25 South Main Street. (Ball.)

In 1926, the Asheville-Biltmore Hotel opened its doors on the corner of Woodfin and Market Streets. The eight-story redbrick hotel, with limestone trim, offered 100 rooms for guests. (Pack.)

In September 1944, the Asheville-Biltmore Hotel, the George Vanderbilt Hotel, the Battery Park Hotel, and the Grove Park Inn all served as redistribution centers for the military. Soldiers were housed in the hotels for 10 to 14 days while receiving physical exams, paperwork, back pay, and reassignment to noncombat duty. (Ball.)

The Asheville-Biltmore Hotel still stands today at 76 North Market Street, although it is now known as the Altamont Apartments. (Author.)

The new Glen Rock Hotel was built on the site of the previous Glen Rock Hotel, which was torn down in 1930 after being condemned as a hazard. As the area around Depot Street deteriorated, the building soon earned renown as a cathouse, and the area around it gained ill repute because of its reputation for gambling and liquor. (Pack.)

The new Glen Rock Hotel is now looking forward to a repurposed future on Depot Street. (Author.)

A parade passes in front of the Asheville Hotel, located at 55 Haywood Street. (Pack.)

Originally built in 1912 as the Elks Home, the Asheville Hotel was designed by the architectural firm of Richard Sharp Smith, the supervising architect of the Biltmore Estate. In 1932, it officially became the Asheville Hotel. (Ball.)

The view down Walnut Street from Haywood Street was a little less crowded in the 1960s before large parking garages were built on Rankin Avenue. (Pack.)

The former Asheville Hotel is now home to the popular Malaprop's Bookstore/Cafe. (Author.)

Seven

THE LONG DEPRESSION

In the late 1920s, the previously flourishing real estate market collapsed. Businesses changed hands rapidly as investors lost money and faith. According to city directories, the hotel at 436 Depot Street had a different name every year between 1928 and 1932: the Hotel Asheville, the Lee Hotel, the Walter Hotel, the Hotel Asheville again, and then the Nantahala. By 1930, a total of 230 stores and 1,800 homes lay vacant in Asheville.

The country entered the Great Depression with the stock market crash of 1929, and, within a year, most of the major banks in Asheville had closed, starting with the Central Bank & Trust. At that time, Asheville had the highest debt in the state and the highest per capita debt in the country. Most of this debt was brought on by projects aimed at making the city more attractive to visitors, such as the new city hall (1928), Pritchard Park (1931), and the Beaucatcher Tunnel (1930). But Asheville had taken on more debt than it could handle, and the banks and the city falsified the securities backing up those municipal bonds. Multiple bank and government officials were indicted after the collapse, leading to the suicides of a former mayor and a bank officer, as well as a prison term for the president of the Central Bank & Trust.

Asheville resolved to pay back every penny it owed in bonds, which took until 1976. During this period, there was little growth because funds were limited, but this stagnation unwittingly led to the preservation of many buildings that may have otherwise been replaced with more modern structures. Because of the long Depression, Asheville now has a collection of Art Deco buildings second only to Miami Beach, and many other historical structures were spared from urban renewal's wrecking ball. The population during this time also stagnated, growing by only 3,000 people between 1930 and 1950.

Asheville's wealthiest family, the Vanderbilts, were also affected by the crash. In 1930, George Vanderbilt's daughter Cornelia decided to open the Biltmore Estate to the public, hoping to generate revenue not only for the grand, expensive house but also for the city of Asheville.

In 1936, one of Asheville's oldest hotels, the Swannanoa, located at 49–51 Biltmore Avenue, became the Milner Hotel. In 1942, a fire damaged the hotel. (Pack.)

The Milner Hotel was a fixture in downtown Asheville from 1936 to 1948, when it became the Earle Hotel. (Pack.)

In 1946, the Milner was renovated, the large moose head above the fireplace was removed, and the furniture was updated in the lobby and the guest rooms. (Pack.)

The Colonial Inn was located at 102 Merrimon Avenue, in a residential part of Asheville that was growing into the tourist trade. The people posing in front of the inn are leaving Asheville after a nice stay in the 1930s. (Pack.)

Built in 1909 as a private residence by Dr. Carl V. Reynolds, the Albemarle Inn at 86 Edgemont Road was used as a school from 1920 to 1941, when it was sold to T. Avery and Marie Taylor. It has functioned as an inn ever since 1941, through six separate owners. (Pack.)

Hungarian composer Béla Bartók stayed at the Albemarle Inn during the winter of 1943–1944. He composed "Sonata for Solo Violin" at the inn. (Pack.)

The former Swannanoa, Swannanoa-Berkeley, and then Milner Hotel became the Earle Hotel in 1948. Located at the corner of Biltmore Avenue and Aston Street, it was demolished in 1968 to make way for a municipal parking lot. (Pack.)

Asheville has had multiple Windsor Hotels located along what are now Biltmore Avenue and Broadway. In 1902, there was a Windsor on North Main Street (now Broadway), and the 1914 city directory lists a Windsor at 48 South Main Street (now Biltmore Avenue). In 1960, another Windsor Hotel was built at 36 Broadway, which is seen here in 1978. (Pack.)

Until recently, the Windsor Hotel, at 36 Broadway, served as a residential hotel. (Author.)

As part of the Jim Crow South, Asheville had segregated hotels until the 1960s. Black hotels included the Savoy, at 33–35 South Market Street, the St. Paul, at 44 Southside Avenue, and the Stoney Front Tourist Home, at 18 Clingman Avenue. These hotels are listed separately in the city directories. This photograph was taken by Andrea Clark. (Pack.)

This photograph by Andrea Clark shows Elijah Morgan in the entrance to the diner of the Savoy Hotel, on the corner of Eagle and Market Streets. (Pack.)

Located at 409 1/2 Southside Avenue, the Booker T. Washington Hotel is listed as a "colored hotel" in the city directory. The Booker T. Washington, seen here in an Andrea Clark photograph, had a popular dance hall that welcomed world-class musicians such as Nat King Cole and Count Basie. In the 1951 directory, it is listed as the James Keyes Hotel. (Pack.)

For years, Asheville, as well as much of the country, dealt with a society that was separate and not treated equally. Until after the Civil Rights Act was passed in the mid-1960s, Asheville was segregated, and "colored" businesses were designated and listed separately in the city directory. Hotels like the James Keyes, seen here in an Andrea Clark photograph, catered to black travelers and remained business fixtures in the black community for years after segregation ended. (Pack.)

When baseball teams from the Negro Leagues came to town, they were welcomed at Rabbit's Hotel, which was famous for its soul food, especially the fried chicken. (Author.)

Eight

MOTOR INNS

After World War II, families began traveling more by automobile, moving business away from the center of the city to the highways just outside. In Asheville, commerce began expanding down Tunnel Road and out on both sides of Highway 25. Thanks in part to Great Smoky Mountains National Park and the Blue Ridge Parkway, Asheville remained a popular place to travel, and many middle-class families who could now afford to take trips flocked to Asheville with their children, opting to stay at places with color television, air-conditioning, and heated pools.

The term *motel* was coined in 1925 and entered into the American lexicon after World War II. It was a condensed form of "motor hotels," meaning that they offered lodging to those traveling by car. They were also called motor inns, motor lodges, motor courts, cabin courts, auto courts, and multiple other names, and they all held the same common traits: they were easily accessible and inexpensive, had outside doors as opposed to inside hallways, were located on highways, and had parking lots. Hotels, on the other hand, had traditionally been downtown or near train depots, and catered to a clientele that did not need to park.

There were no parlors or ballrooms for large social gatherings in motels. Meals were also not included, but some motels, like the Howard Johnson, had a restaurant attached. Families could also find affordable dining at drive-ins, such as Bucks, Wink's, or Babe Maloy's, which were all popular restaurants on Tunnel Road in the 1950s.

After the regional airport was built in 1961 and the interstate highway system through the mountains completed in 1966, the need for passenger trains diminished. In the 1970s, after passenger service ended, the railway depot, which had been the gateway to Asheville for tourists for 90 years, was demolished.

Most motels had their heyday in the 1960s, but Asheville is lucky to still have many of them, such as the iconic Mountaineer Inn on Tunnel Road and the Pines and the Log Cabin Court on Highway 25.

Located at 1 Flint Street, next to the auditorium, the Auditorium Hotel Court had 50 rooms, all equipped with radios and telephones, when it opened in 1951. (Pack.)

The Tour-O-Tel Motor Court was opened in 1942 at 640 Merrimon Avenue. It was run by Ray Winkwerder and offered guests a comfortable and affordable place to stay just north of downtown Asheville. (Pack.)

Thunder Road, a 1958 blockbuster starring Robert Mitchum, filmed scenes at the Log Cabin Motor Court, located north of Asheville on Highway 25. Colonel Sanders, of Kentucky Fried Chicken fame, owned a motor court up the road as well. (Pack.)

In the 1950s and 1960s, Tunnel Road sprouted motels, shops, and restaurants. It was a popular place to "cruise," and is still a good value for tourists, with its proximity to downtown Asheville and its profusion of shopping and dining choices. The Blue Ridge Motor Lodge is located near the Beaucatcher Tunnel the road is named for. (Author.)

Howard Johnson's was the most popular restaurant chain in the country in the 1960s and 1970s. It first began expanding its business into motor lodges in the 1950s. The first Howard Johnson's motel opened in Savannah, Georgia, in 1954. The chain came to 29 Tunnel Road in Asheville in 1956. (Pack.)

Howard Johnson's operated on Tunnel Road from 1956 to 1970. (Pack.)

The Mountaineer Inn opened in 1948 and still hangs its iconic neon signs along Tunnel Road, just through Beaucatcher Tunnel from downtown Asheville. (Author.)

DISCOVER THOUSANDS OF LOCAL HISTORY BOOKS
FEATURING MILLIONS OF VINTAGE IMAGES

Arcadia Publishing, the leading local history publisher in the United States, is committed to making history accessible and meaningful through publishing books that celebrate and preserve the heritage of America's people and places.

Find more books like this at
www.arcadiapublishing.com

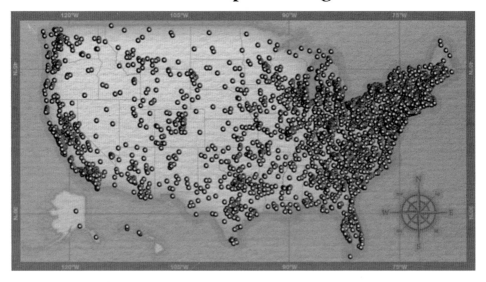

Search for your hometown history, your old stomping grounds, and even your favorite sports team.

Consistent with our mission to preserve history on a local level, this book was printed in South Carolina on American-made paper and manufactured entirely in the United States. Products carrying the accredited Forest Stewardship Council (FSC) label are printed on 100 percent FSC-certified paper.

MADE IN THE USA